T0209440

GIVE ME RECOVERY OR GIVE ME DEATH

The Direction Home

by

Progress Anonymous

BALBOA
PRESS

A DIVISION OF HAY HOUSE

Balboa Press books may be ordered through booksellers or by contacting:

Balboa Press
A Division of Hay House
1663 Liberty Drive
Bloomington, IN 47403
www.balboapress.com
1 (877) 407-4847

Print information available on the last page.

Library of Congress Control Number: 2018914790

ISBN: 978-1-9822-1805-8 (sc)
ISBN: 978-1-9822-1804-1 (e)

Balboa Press rev. date: 09/06/2019

Give Me Recovery
or
Give Me Death
will empower you
to help yourself,
and those close to you,
with your addictions.

You will improve
yourself, and
improve your life.

For the people in recovery (the tip of the iceberg) and the people who would probably benefit substantially from recovery, in the tens of millions, at least.

ACKNOWLEDGMENTS

I have already acknowledged and thanked the people who normally would be put here.

In keeping with the spirit of anonymity, I will say nothing specific about them in this book.

To those unnamed and unexplained people, thank you again for your help, moral support, and love. It's appreciated and returned.

CONTENTS

GIVE ME RECOVERY
OR
GIVE ME DEATH
The Direction Home

PRELIMINARY CONCEPTS
PART 1

"A SECOND CHANCE AT A FIRST-CLASS LIFE."

"Sobriety and recovery will make you about the best person you can be.

Alcohol will make you about the worst."

"AA (Alcoholics Anonymous) will give you a second chance at a first-class life."

"With recovery you get promoted.

Without recovery you get fired (or worse)."

"Know recovery, know peace.

No recovery, no peace (or worse)."

OVER 55 12-STEP PROGRAMS.

There are at least 55 12-step recovery programs. Many people say it's over 100. Apparently, each has its own meetings, often with its own literature.

The other programs use the same 12 steps, usually only replacing in step 1 alcohol (AA), with our addiction (NA), cocaine (CA), or nicotine (NicA), for some examples.

Replace for yourself your own issue(s).

"PROGRAMS OF HOPE."

The 12 traditions of AA are used by all or most of the other 12-step programs, changing OA for AA, or eating compulsively for drinking, for two examples.

"The 12-step programs are programs of hope:

Hope....good (prolongs life).

No hope....bad (shortens life)."

Hope:

"Hang on pain ends."

"Helping other people every day."

"Hearing other people's experiences."

"FROM A SEEMINGLY HOPELESS STATE OF MIND AND BODY...."

Newcomer: "So what are we recovering from?"

Sober old timer: "Everything."

Newcomer: "Be serious."

Sober old timer: "I am. Ok, according to the Big Book, *Alcoholics Anonymous,* we are recovering from a seemingly hopeless state of mind and body, a state of pitiful, incomprehensible, demoralization."

"I DESERVE A DRINK."

A too common story:

A fellow has done his program faithfully for 20 plus years. He had no alcohol. He attended meetings regularly. He worked on the steps. He had been in service.

One not so fine day, he said to himself: "I deserve a drink." He had a drink which led to a two-week binge which ended with him killing several people while driving drunk.

His next stop will probably be prison for multiple years.

OTHER 12-STEP PROGRAMS.

Here are some other 12-step programs besides AA:

Narcotics Anonymous (NA).

Cocaine Anonymous (CA).

Nicotine Anonymous (NicA).

Overeaters Anonymous (OA).

Marijuana Anonymous (MA).

Adult Children of Alcoholics (ACA).

Debtors Anonymous (DA).

Bloggers Anonymous (BA).

Al-Anon.

"YOU HAVE TO KNOW SOMEONE."

"Al-Anon is for the people close to the Alcoholic or Alcoholics, to help the Al-Anons cope, improve themselves, and improve their lives."

"AA welcomes anyone, no matter how down and out.

For Al-Anon, you have to know someone."

Al-Anon is not a support group for guys named Al.

THEY STAYED FOR THE THINKING.

From AA (Alcoholics Anonymous):
"We came for the drinking, we stayed for the thinking."

"So what's an addiction?"
"A bad habit."
Again, "So what's an addiction?"
"A bad habit."

"We may or may not be responsible for our addictions and or our character defects (same things   ?), but we are responsible for our recoveries."

THEY STAYED FOR THE SANITY.

From OA (Overeaters Anonymous):
"We came for the vanity, we stayed for the sanity."

"If you find yourself in the lane where cars come toward you, don't wait until tomorrow to pull over."

"Service is slimming."

IT WAS A RESCUE.

From NA (Narcotics Anonymous):

"It wasn't an arrest, it was a rescue."

"No one ever came into recovery on a winning streak, but many people have gone out (relapsed) on winning streaks."

"I preferred cocaine, I liked the smell."

"NA — never again, never alone." (Many/most addictions are diseases of isolation.)

"I came into NA penniless, homeless, and jobless. Now I have a job that sends me all around the world, and not always to get rid of me."

"MEETINGS ARE THE HEARTBEATS OF THE 12-STEP PROGRAMS."

"Meetings are the heartbeats of the 12-step programs."

"Go to meetings. Don't drink between meetings. If you have a problem with that, go to more meetings."

From MA (Marijuana Anonymous):
"Keep off the grass."
"You have to feel to heal."

A PROGRAM OF HUMILITY.

Newcomer: "Can you summarize the AA program in one word?"

Sober old timer: "Yes."

Newcomer: "What word? And enough with the attempted humor."

Sober old timer: "Humility, and that's just my opinion."

(More on humility later.)

"Your greatest asset in recovery is how bad it was (to a point)."

"A DAILY REPRIEVE."

"We have a daily reprieve based upon the maintenance of our spiritual condition."

Usually the sober old timers attribute their sobriety to one day at a time. Some sober old timers attribute their sobriety to one moment at a time.

"There are no days off in AA."

SPIRITUAL PROGRAMS,
NOT RELIGIOUS PROGRAMS.

Newcomer: "AA is supposed to be a spiritual program, not a religious program. What's the difference?"

Sober old timer: "Religion is for people who don't want to go to hell. Spirituality is for people who have been to hell and don't want to go back."

"AA is the people's therapy."

FOR PEOPLE
WHO WANT THE MEAL.

"You want the meal, do the deal."

"What's the meal?"

"Sobriety.

Peace.

Self-improvement.

Success, and so on."

FOR PEOPLE
WHO DO THE DEAL.

"What's the deal?"

"Stay sober.

Attend meetings.

Do the steps.

Read the literature.

Be of service, and so on."

"You can't change the past, but you can change the future."

DENIAL

"If you're in only one 12-step program, you're in denial."

Not you're in the Nile, you're in denial. (You might be in the Nile, but what are the odds?)

"Denial:
Don't even notice I am lying."

"A DESIGN FOR RIGHT LIVING."

"AA provides a design for right living. It's practically a manual for right living."

"What you put in front of your recovery you will lose."

Here's an accomplishment for you:

"When I was in my addiction, I was named employee of the month, and I was fired by the same company, in the same month."

"IT'S NOT ALCOHOLWASM."

"It's not alcoholwasm.
It's alcoholism."

The ism:
"I sabotage myself."
"Incredibly short memory."

"We are not responsible for our thoughts, but we are responsible for our actions and our spoken and written words."

"90% OF SUCCESS IS JUST SHOWING UP."

Woody Allen supposedly said: "90% of success is just showing up."

"Suit up, show up, and grow up."

In AA:

"When you leave a meeting, know when your next meeting will be. Always know when your next meeting will be."

In OA:

"When you finish your meal, know when your next meal will be. Always know when your next meal will be.

Also, always know when your next meeting will be."

RULE # 1.

"Rule #1: Meetings, meetings, meetings.

Rule #2: See rule #1."

The usual advice to newcomers:

"Go to 90 meetings in 90 days. After that, just go to a meeting a day."

Of the first 90 meetings (hopefully in 90 days) try to go to mostly speaker/discussion meetings at 7 to 10 different places, if possible.

"KEEP COMING BACK."

"Can I go to AA if alcohol is not my problem or my main problem?"

"Yes. Also try NA. Judges often send heroin addicts, crank addicts, oxycodone addicts, alcoholics, etc., to AA or NA or both; the people can go to whichever they prefer."

Here's one approach:

Start by saying you just want to listen. In AA you can call yourself an alcoholic. In NA you can call yourself an addict.

The people will tell you to "keep coming back."

"THOUGHTFUL INTROSPECTION."

"The unexamined life is not worth living." (Attributed to Socrates)

"Knowing yourself is the beginning of all wisdom." (Attributed to Aristotle)

"If you don't go within, you'll go without."

"Thoughtless….bad.

Thoughtful….good.

Introspection….good."

"AA, NA, and so on are programs of thoughtful introspection."

"If you've got a drinking problem, don't drink. If you've got a thinking problem, get into AA ASAP."

"AA is the people's therapy."

"AA will show you the direction home and will give you a new home."

"YOU'RE RIGHT."

Newcomer: "I presume that my odds will be better if I go to a lot of meetings."

Sober old timer: "You're right."

Newcomer: "I presume most relapses occur when people stop going to meetings."

Sober old timer: "You're right."

Newcomer: "I presume that I can go to too many meetings."

Sober old timer: "You're right."

Newcomer: "You say you're right a lot."

Sober old timer: "You're right."

PRELIMINARY CONCEPTS
PART 2

HE KEPT COMING BACK.

One sober old timer, who died in his 80's of natural causes, said often at meetings in the last year of his life: "The only thing I did right in my last 27 years (how long he had been sober) was that I kept coming back."

Other members: "Wherever I went before AA, I was told to not come back. In AA I've always been told to keep coming back."

"MEETING MAKERS MAKE IT."

Most 12-step meetings last for an hour or an hour and a half, sometimes with a brief break.

"Meetings are insurance against the first drink."

"Meeting makers make it."

"People go to meetings to find out what happens to people who don't go to meetings."

SPEAKER/DISCUSSION MEETINGS.

There are two kinds of meetings:

1) Speaker/discussion meetings.

2) The rest, mostly book studies.

In the speaker/discussion meetings, the speaker shares his or her experience, strength, and hope, followed by a discussion on a topic of the speaker's choice.

My opinion: The first 10 meetings plus should be speaker/discussion meetings.

Newcomer: "Why are the speakers encouraged to stand when they speak?"

Sober old timer: "They lie less; just a little humor, or attempt anyway."

THE BS METER.

Often a timer is used to give more people a chance to share; you can always say you'd prefer to listen. The timer, usually set for three minutes, is aka the bs meter.

Dr. Bob, one of the two cofounders of AA, supposedly said: "Not counting the speaker, any share longer than five minutes is ego."

The speaker/discussion meetings have the secretary and the speaker sitting up front. The book studies have only the secretary sitting up front.

DON'T DRINK AND DON'T SCREW UP.

"Any day that I don't drink is a good day."

"Any day that I don't screw up is a good day."

AA was the first 12-step program and is still the largest by far. I'm not the only person who will tell you that its cofounders, Bill W and Dr. Bob, were two of the great men of the 20th century, or any century for that matter.

BILL GOT SOBER FIRST.

Bill W was hospitalized four times in 1934 for alcohol-related health issues like vomiting blood and or inability to stop drinking alcohol. His first day of permanent sobriety was in December 1934.

It took him six months to permanently sober up another alcoholic, Dr. Bob. People in recovery are usually very grateful for Bill's remarkable persistence, insight, and writing skill.

AA'S BIRTHDAY.

AA's birthday is considered to be Dr. Bob's first day of permanent sobriety, on June 10, 1935, in Akron, Ohio.

Dr. Bob was tremendous at sobering up "wet" alcoholics and bringing them into the fellowship. He personally saved the lives of thousands of alcoholics.

THEY WERE BOTH FROM....
VERMONT.

Bill W and Dr. Bob were a very good team. They supposedly never exchanged harsh words with each other. They were both from....Vermont.

The first edition of our book, *Alcoholics Anonymous*, written by Bill W, came out in 1939. As the story goes, it was printed on very thick paper, making it a big book, giving it its unofficial name, the Big Book.

THE EDITIONS OF THE BIG BOOK.

The four editions of the Big Book:
Edition 1: 1939....100 members.
Edition 2: 1955....150,000-plus members
with meetings in 50 countries.
Edition 3: 1976....1 million-plus members
with meetings in 90 countries.
Edition 4: 2001....2 million-plus members
with meetings in 150 countries.

(Each edition contains the total members and usually the total countries that the meetings are held in, approximate for both.)

For your information, the original title of the Big Book was .... *The Way Out.*

THE BIRTHPLACE OF AA:
AKRON, OHIO.

How many steps were there and are there up to Dr. Bob's house in Akron, Ohio, now open to the public?

You guessed it, or maybe you didn't....12.

The first three AA groups started in the mid-1930s in order:

1) Akron, Ohio.

2) New York, New York.

3) Cleveland, Ohio.

REST IN PEACE.

Dr. Bob, cofounder of AA
August 8, 1879 - November 16, 1950
Died from colon cancer at age 71.

REST IN PEACE.

Bill W, cofounder of AA
November 26, 1895 - January 24, 1971
Died from emphysema at age 75.

REST IN PEACE.

"MY ADDICTION IS VERY BAD FOR ME."

Step 1 of NA (There are 12 steps officially.):

We admitted we were powerless over our addiction—that our lives (not our wives, our lives) had become unmanageable.

If powerless is not quite the right word for you, try this:

"My addiction is very bad for me."

Sponsor: "What do you do if you are hungry and only have lemons?"

Sponsee: "Make lemonade?"

Sponsor: "Don't tell me you like lemonade. Order a pizza."

"FULLY SELF-SUPPORTING."

Tradition 7 of NA (There are 12 traditions officially.):

Every NA group ought to be fully self-supporting, declining outside contributions.

AA, for example, is entirely self-supporting through the voluntary contributions of its members, usually one or two dollars per member per meeting. The money helps pay for the rent, the literature, the coffee, the hot air, the electricity, and so on.

A BETTER PERSON
AND A BETTER GROUP.

The 12 steps and the 12 traditions (pages 199 and 200) are read at most meetings. The steps will make you a better person; the traditions will make your group a better group.

The traditions have been tested. They don't require much thought or explanation. Try to follow them.

"REALITY, WHAT A CONCEPT."

"Sobriety....good.

Drinking....bad."

"The sober life is so much simpler, easier, productive, and better."

"Sober: Son of a bitch, everything's real."

"Reality, what a concept."

"You don't have to drink today."

"Yesterday is gone and tomorrow will never come."

"WHAT'S A SLIP?"

"What's a slip?"
"Sobriety loses its priority."

Dr. Bob supposedly said (back in the day):
"Underneath every dress is a slip."

"One drink is too many and 100 is not enough."
"If you don't have the first drink, you can't get drunk."

"GET OFF THE PITY POT, WE NEED THE POT."

"Poor me.

Poor me.

Pour me another drink."

"Get off the cross, we need the wood."

"Get off the pity pot, we need the pot."

"Man takes drink.

  Drink takes drink.

  Drink takes man."

"If you get killed by a train, it's not the caboose that kills you (unless it's moving backwards)."

TWO BARTENDERS TALKING.

Veteran bartender: "How can you tell the guy who is having a relapse after months of sobriety in AA?"

New bartender: "Enlighten me."

Veteran bartender: "He's the guy who orders 12 drinks, gives away the first, and drinks the rest. He thinks the first drink is the one that will kill him."

"AA IS A WE PROGRAM."

"AA is a we program."

"You don't have to do it alone."

"You can't do it alone."

"The first word of the first step is we."

"If you turn the W upside down, you get me."

"We + ll = well.

I + ll = ill."

MORE THAN RAINBOWS, ROSES, AND THE YELLOW BRICK ROAD.

The AA program is more than rainbows, roses, and the yellow brick road. There's work to be done:

The steps, among several other things like meetings and the literature.

Just a few words about the steps now, more later.

Here's an acronym:

"Nuts — not using the steps."

"DO THE STEPS OR DIE."

One rather intimidating looking, bulky guy (from working out), who had been incarcerated several times, with tattoos and earrings, said this at a meeting in a deep, loud voice: "Do the steps or die, mother fu--ers."

I find it motivating. Maybe you had to be there.

"TAKE THE STEPS TO GET BACK UP."

"You can take the elevator, fall down the shaft, or get the shaft, to reach your bottom, but you have to take the steps to get back up."

It's also said:

"You reach your bottom when you stop digging."

A blackout story:

"I went to my usual bar. The bartender said rudely that last night, when he threw me out, he told me not to come back for a few months. Well, excuse me!!"

HE'S STILL A HORSE THIEF.

Here's a predicament the steps should help:

"I used to be a drunk and a horse thief. Now I don't drink, but I'm still a horse thief and I'm supposed to return the horse."

"You want to feel better, go to meetings.

You want to get better, do the steps."

Do both.

FOR CERTAIN BACK PROBLEMS, DO THE STEPS.

Here's another predicament the steps should help:

"I'm here for my back problems. I want my wife back, my family back, my job back, my driver's license back, my car back. There's more, but you get the picture."

Here's another accomplishment for you:

"After five years of sobriety, I had a relapse and I took some time off from work. On my first day back to work, I was fired, still in my relapse, and it was just half a day."

THE SPIRITUAL PRINCIPLES BEHIND THE STEPS AND THE TRADITIONS.

"The spiritual principle behind the steps is humility.

The spiritual principle behind the traditions is anonymity."

"The steps are suicide prevention.

The traditions are homicide prevention."

YOU CAN PICK
YOUR OWN HIGHER POWER.

A few words about your higher power:

If the God of your childhood or your current God works for you, stay with your God.

If not, you can decide on your own higher power.

"Trust God.

Clean house.

Be of service."

IDEAS FOR YOUR HIGHER POWER.

Here are some other ideas for your higher power:

"Gift of desperation.

Good.

Good orderly direction.

Grace over drugs.

Great outdoors.

Great spirit.

Group of drunks (in recovery).

The AA, NA, or ACA programs or any other.

The 12 steps (as is, or with your modifications)."

"IF I HAD TO STAY WITH
THE GOD OF MY CHILDHOOD...."

A lady with many years of sobriety and meetings: "If I had to stay with the God of my childhood, I doubt I'd still be here."

"It's up to you to decide on your higher power.

But don't pick the doorknob; it will turn on you."

"Picking your higher power:
What a concept."

"EGO IS EDGING GOD OUT."

"Trust God.
Clean house.
Be of service."

"The answer is God, what's the question?"

I repeat, "The answer is God, what's the question?"

"Ego is edging God out."

"God and ego can't live in the same house at the same time."

"My ego is not my amigo."

"CLEAN AND SERENE"

We turn the peer pressure around, from "Come on, it's the Fourth of July, since when do you say no to good cocaine?" to, after four months of AA meetings where sobriety is endorsed, sitting in front of the fire with your family on Thanksgiving eve, drinking warm apple cider, "clean and serene," with the bills paid.

"We're proud of you."

"Don't leave until the miracle happens."

"WE OFFER SUGGESTIONS ONLY."

The steps, the traditions, the advice of the members, the literature, etc., are suggestions only.

"You don't have to do anything in AA. We offer suggestions only."

Sponsor: "Why think outside the box?"
Sponsee: "Tell me."
Sponsor: "The box is in pretty bad shape."

"WE CLEAN UP OUR SIDE OF THE STREET."

"We spend the first half of our lives screwing it up and the second half trying to clean it up."

"We clean up our side of the street."

"Two wrongs don't make a right."

"If you think you have a better idea than your 12-step program(s), go for it. We'll refund your misery at the door.

If your idea doesn't work out so well for you, just come back. You won't be the first person, nor the last person, to leave and come back."

(Your ego won't be happy. Ignore it.)

THE SLOGANS

FROM FIVE TO SIX SLOGANS.

Here come six of the best slogans in recovery. They are on the walls, in their frames, of many recovery meeting rooms. They started out as five, but the first word of each forms a slogan, which may be the best, making six slogans.

The first word of each of the five slogans:

"Live easy, but think first."

"LIVE EASY, BUT THINK FIRST."

Usually:

"LIVE and let live.

EASY does it.

BUT for the grace of God go I.

THINK, think, think.

FIRST things first."

"Learn to listen.

Listen to learn."

HER SECRET TO HER LONGEVITY.

"Live and let live:"

A good policy to live by.

A lady 102 years old from Chicago (remember Al Capone) said her secret to her longevity was: "I mind my own business."

"Live and let live:"

Did you know that the James Bond film starring Roger Moore, released in 1973, described as "high octane 007 suspense," was called "Live and let die?"

"Live and let live" has been a mainstream quotation for years.

"THERE BUT FOR THE GRACE OF GOD GO I."

"Easy does it:"

Words to live by.

"Just do it."

"But for the grace of God go I."

One worker told a coworker about another coworker who, while driving drunk, caused a car accident, got seriously injured, seriously injured several other people, did extensive property damage, and was taken to the hospital. After the hospital, he may go directly to jail, if he's still alive.

The coworker who heard the story replied: "There but for the grace of God go I."

WHAT'S A YET?

If you have partaken in a lot of alcohol and or other mind-altering substances, have frequently driven while under the influence, and never injured anyone else or yourself, we call that "a yet....you're eligible too."

"My ego is not my amigo."

"THINK BEFORE YOU DRINK."

"Think, think, think."

For starters:

"Think before you drink."

"Look before you leap."

"Think, think, think" was apparently used by IBM back in the day.

"MAYBE IT'S NOT SUCH A GREAT IDEA."

"The first think: I think I have a great idea.

The second think: Maybe it's not such a great idea.

The third think: Forget it."

"Keep thinking, try not to do any-thing."

"Don't just do something, sit there."

"Think it through to the end."

PRIORITIZE.

"First things first."

Prioritize:

"First things first.

Second things second.

Third things third."

Newcomer: "So what is the first thing?"

Sober old timer: "For us—don't drink."

The problem drinker or drug user has about 3 possible fates:

Get locked up.

Get covered up.

Get sobered up.

"DON'T THROW THE BABY OUT WITH THE BATHWATER."

"Take what you like and leave the rest."

You will probably find most of your recovery program very helpful and lifesaving, but you disagree with a few points. That's OK. That's good. But "don't throw the baby out with the bathwater."

"Take what you like (the baby, and or most of the program), and leave the rest."

"ODAAT, OMAAT AND KISS."

"One day at a time. ODAAT."
Notice there are two A's. For AA?

"I've got my double-digit sobriety because I didn't drink and I didn't die, one day at a time."

"ODAAT: One day at a time."

"OMAAT: One moment at a time."

"KISS: Keep it simple stupid. Simplify."

SHE'S GETTING BETTER.

"Progress, not perfection."

One lady: "I'm getting better. First, I was a drunk. Then I was an alcohol enthusiast. Now I'm an alcoholic."

"Rome wasn't built in a day."

"Give time time."

Give yourself a break. Consider forgetting perfection, unless you are a neurosurgeon.

"Easy does it."

"Progress, not perfection."

"THIS TOO SHALL PASS."

Here's a beautiful and profound rock song that explains it better than I can:

"All Things Must Pass," by George Harrison, released in 1970.

On YouTube, type in and watch:

Harrison All Things Must pass.

(No song lyrics are printed in this book due to concerns about copyright infringement. Sorry.)

"This too shall pass" is usually the AA way to put it.

MORE ABOUT RECOVERY

THE DIRECTION HOME.

Rolling Stone magazine called the song, "Like a Rolling Stone," by Bob Dylan, released in 1965, the greatest rock song of the 20th century.

One of the biographies of Bob Dylan, written by Robert Shelton, is called: *No Direction Home* (mentioned in the above song).

Recovery shows you the direction home, and gives you a new home.

Type and watch on YouTube:

Mellencamp Like a Rolling Stone. (This is a tremendous version; watch it.)

"AN EXTRA MOMENT'S PAUSE."

"We pause when agitated or doubtful."

"Nothing is more helpful than restraint of pen and tongue (usually)."

"For every year in recovery, we get an extra moment's pause, on average."

To repeat, "For every year in recovery, we get an extra moment's pause, on average."

"THE SLIPPERY SLOPE."

"Insanity is doing the same thing over and over again and expecting different results."

One drink will put the real alcoholic on "the slippery slope." Perhaps 90 percent of the time, he will get drunk and eventually pass out.

"When drunk, I don't fall asleep, I pass out.

Also, when drunk, I don't wake up, I come to."

"YOUR DRUG OF NO CHOICE."

"Before recovery, your preferred substance was not your drug of choice, it was your drug of no choice."

"Don't have the first drink."
"Stay out of slippery places."

"So what is a pipe dream?"
"A delusional dream after smoking something mind-altering in a pipe, like marijuana or heroin."

NARROW THE ROAD.

"The road narrows."

One small problem: You've got to narrow the road for yourself. You will. The sooner the better. (Do less, say less, stay home more, get more sleep, etc.)

The topic at a speaker/discussion meeting was: "What are you doing today to maintain or improve your spiritual condition?"

One answer: "I stay sober, I am attending a meeting, I work on the steps, I pray, I meditate, I read from the literature, and I read from my own notes."

It sounds like that person is on the right track.

"DON'T PRESS YOUR LUCK."

"It's recovery or Russian roulette."

"Don't press your luck."

"Quit while you're ahead." (At least you're still alive.)

"AA is the last house on the block."

For us, it might be the only safe house on the block.

"Alcohol and recovery are cunning, baffling, and powerful.

They are also progressive."

BE HONEST WITH YOURSELF.

"Honesty is about being honest with yourself."

Be honest with yourself. With others, it's "progress, not perfection."

Worry first about being honest with yourself.

"Honesty (at least with yourself) is the best policy."

"HONESTY WITHOUT COMPASSION."

"Honesty without compassion is brutality."

"Kind thoughts.
Kind words.
Kind deeds."

"You can get (practically) anything you want, if you help enough people get what they want."

"WHAT YOU'RE NOT GRATEFUL FOR."

"What you're not grateful for, you will lose."

"What you put in front of your recovery, you will lose."

Many people are very grateful for their programs of recovery. They also practically swear by their daily gratitude lists.

"LASTLY, IT WAS JUST CONSEQUENCES."

"First it was fun.

Then it was fun and consequences.

Lastly, it was just consequences."

"Alcohol started out as the solution. When it became the problem, I really had a problem."

"The only things worse than my problems are my solutions."

WHY NOT GO
TO THE WINNING SIDE?

Sober old timer: "We think to surrender is to go to the winning side."

Newcomer: "What's the winning side?"

Sober old timer: "For most of us, it's the side with our higher power. We surrendered to our higher power, which could be the AA or NA programs or the 12 steps, among many other things. (See page 53.) Also included — almost always, of course — is sobriety."

ACCEPTANCE AND EXPECTATIONS.

"Acceptance....good.

Expectations....bad."

Newcomer: "What are the two most important things to accept?"

Sober old timer: "We cannot have the first drink and our higher power; not necessarily in that order, and that's just my opinion.

Also, watch out for the expectations:

Increased expectations....decreased serenity.

Decreased expectations....increased serenity."

FIX THE OFF SWITCH.

Usually we are addicted to more and our off switches are broken.

It's better to fix the off switch than wait for the car to run out of gas.

Ya think?

AA is often referred to as:

"An attitude adjustment."

"Awareness and acceptance."

"HASTE MAKES WASTE (USUALLY)."

"Haste makes waste."

"Careful….good.

Careless….bad."

"An ounce of prevention is worth a pound of cure."

(Attributed to Benjamin Franklin)

Don't forget, usually "there are at least two sides to every story."

"I've got recovery without (without the possibility of parole), as opposed to some inmates who have life without."

AVOID A GREAT FALL.

"Humpty Dumpty sat on the wall. Humpty Dumpty had a great fall. All the king's horses and all the king's men couldn't put Humpty Dumpty together again."

OK, be careful not to have a great fall. I repeat, be careful not to have a great fall.

But why include the king's horses? Have they ever put anything together again? Why not all the king's women and all the king's men....?

WHAT IS INSANITY?

"Insanity is doing the same thing over and over and expecting different results."

"If you don't have a resentment with someone in the rooms, you're not going to enough meetings."

So, if you go to a lot of meetings, don't be surprised and or upset with a new resentment with someone in the rooms. It's practically inevitable.

"DON'T LEAVE
UNTIL THE MIRACLE HAPPENS."

A lady in recovery: "We will love you until you learn to love yourself. Don't leave until the miracle happens.

After that, keep coming back."

"Expectations….bad.

They are future resentments, or resentments under construction."

Words to a sponsor: "You can lead a horse to water, but you can't make him drink, or not drink."

"WHO IS WISE?"

"Who is wise?"

"A person who learns from everyone."

Again, "Who is wise?"

"A person who learns from everyone."

Most members wish they crawled into recovery way before they did. At least they did. "Better late than never."

"LEARN FROM OTHER PEOPLE'S MISTAKES."

"Not learning from your mistakes …. very bad.

Learning from your mistakes …. good.

Learning from other people's mistakes …. very good."

In front of the main branch of the New York Public Library are statues of two lions. One represents patience. The other represents fortitude. Did they have AA meetings at that library back in the day?

"MY EGO IS NOT MY AMIGO."

"Sometimes humble pie is all there is to eat.

Eat it."

"Let them call me pisha." (A pisha is a child who pees in his pants.)

"My ego is not my amigo."
"Ego in excess....bad.
Humility in excess....bad.
Being right sized....good."

Err towards humility.

"I SCREW UP LESS."

The topic at a night meeting was: "What keeps you coming back?"

One fellow said: "I screw up less. Any day that I don't screw up is a good day."

"The spiritual principle behind the steps is humility.

AA is a program of humility."

Your poop stinks.

Get over it.

"THINK, THINK, THINK."

"Suicide is a permanent solution to an often temporary problem."

"Speed kills."

"We pause when agitated or doubtful."

"Nothing is more helpful than restraint of pen and tongue."

"Think, think, think:

The first think: I think I have a great idea.

The second think: Maybe it's not such a great idea.

The third think: Forget it."

PATIENCE AND IMPATIENCE.

"Give me patience, now!!??"

"Patience….good.
Impatience….bad."

"Give me chastity, but not yet!!??"

"You can't save your face and your butt at the same time (usually)."
First, save your butt.

WHEN YOU GET BAD NEWS.

What is usually the first thing to do when you get seemingly bad news?

Nothing.

What is often the best thing to do when you get seemingly bad news?

Nothing.

That's right, nothing.

A month later you may find that so far so good, and you might continue to do nothing. The news may not have been as bad as you first thought.

"WATCH OUT FOR THE FITS."

"Free time is the devil's workshop."
"Watch out for the fits."
"What are the fits?"
"The fu--its."

"The kiss of death or at least a relapse:
I've got this program. I don't need to go to meetings."

"Stinking thinking leads to drinking."

"CHANGE IS AN INSIDE JOB."

"Geographics (moving often) usually don't work out so well."

Worry more about improving the inner you.

Worry less about improving the outer you. (It will follow.)

"Wherever you go, you'll find the same face in the mirror."

"Change is an inside job."

"If you don't change, you'll be asking for change."

"AA is a program of self-improvement."

RECOVERY HUMOR
OR ATTEMPTS AT.

"How are you?"

"I'm a quart low."

"How many Al-Anons does it take to change a light bulb?"

"None. They disengage and watch it screw itself."

The daughter: "How do I know if a person is drunk?"

The father: "You see the two cars parked across the street, the drunk will tell you that there are four."

The wife: "There is only one car parked across the street."

"SUFFERING IS OPTIONAL."

"Death is inevitable.

Suffering is optional."

"Get off the cross, we need the wood."

"Get off the pity pot, we need the pot."

"Before recovery, your preferred substance was not your drug of choice, it was your drug of no choice."

Just because you like the smell of cocaine is not a good reason to use it.

EVEN MORE ABOUT RECOVERY

DON'T REACT.
IF POSSIBLE, CREATE.

Usually:

"Slow down.

Do less.

Say less.

Think more. (Think everything through, before and after.)

Don't react."

"SLOW DOWN."

"Slow down." It's like you're driving 60 mph in a 15 mph school zone, when school is in session.

If you are driving 60 mph in a 15 mph school zone, when school is in session, and you kill a child who darts out between cars, you'll probably get multiple years in the slammer.

Better to "slow down."
Ya think?
"Speed kills."

WHY HAVE A SPEED-CHESS LIFE?

In speed chess (often called blitz chess) played with chess clocks, players average about eight to 10 seconds per move. One fellow calls speed chess idiot chess. He says it is the way he plays it.

In usual tournament chess, when people average perhaps three minutes per move, his moves are much better. Unfortunately for him, so are his opponents.

Why lead your life like you're playing speed chess?

Why have a speed-chess life?

"DO LESS."

"Do less."

You don't have to and you can't do everything you've ever heard about.

One person, from his first seven attempts to climb Mount Everest, lost nine fingers from frostbite.

On his eighth attempt, he lost his life.

"Do less."

WHEN IN DOUBT.

Usually:

"When in doubt, don't; when not in doubt, get in doubt".

"We're human beings, not human do-ings."

"Do the next right thing (which might be nothing)."

PAUSING AND RESTRAINT.

"We pause when agitated or doubtful."

How bout we always pause, when possible?

"Pausing….(usually) good."

"Nothing is more helpful than restraint of pen and tongue."

How bout we always exercise restraint, when possible?

"Restraint….(usually) good."

"WHY AM I TALKING?"

"Wait:
Why am I talking?"

"Say less."
"Imagine you had to pay $504.28 for every word you spoke."

"Loose lips sink ships."
"I try to never miss an opportunity to shut up."

"BE A GOOD LISTENER."

Sponsor: "Take the cotton out of your ears and put it in your mouth. You've heard it before but it's worth repeating."

Sponsee: "What?"

"We are not a glum lot."

"Think more."

Don't forget the buyer's remorse period, when you can return a mistaken purchase with no strings attached.

"FIRST THOUGHT WRONG."

"Don't react (if possible)."

In case you haven't noticed, your first thoughts are usually wrong, and often illegal. AA wisdom:

"First Thought Wrong."

"A good idea is the enemy of a very good idea."

"I don't trust my own mind."

"We are not responsible for our thoughts but we are responsible for our actions and our spoken and written words."

"DON'T REACT," EVEN IN CELEBRATION, IF POSSIBLE.

A pro golfer hit a hole-in-one. In celebration he dove headfirst into the nearby water trap, which, where he dove, was very shallow. (Get ready for a horrible ending.) He will apparently live out the rest of his life as a quadriplegic — after a hole-in one.

"There but for the grace of God go I."

"Don't react," even in celebration, if possible."

"Learn from other people's mistakes."

"Speed kills."

"PATIENCE IS A VIRTUE."

Don't forget that "there are usually at least two sides to every story."

"Patience is a virtue."

"Don't react (if possible), create."

"For every year in AA, you get an extra moment's pause, on average."

If everyone always acted on their first thoughts, I think we'd all be arrested, or should be, providing we're still alive, and not incarcerated. It might be a crazy idea, but I believe it.

"LET IT BE."

My pick for the most profound and empowering rock song ever (that I've heard): "Let it Be," written by Paul McCartney and John Lennon, first sung by the Beatles, released in 1970.

Type in and watch on YouTube: McCartney Let it be.

"Let it be." Words to live by, usually. You may come up with something good, but probably not right away.

In an effort to leave no stone unturned, I counted the let it bes in one version. There were 39.

Who counts the let it bes, in "Let it be?"

"THE NO-MATTER-WHAT CLUB."

A number of sober old timers attribute their success to belonging to the "no-matter-what club." No matter what, they won't drink.

The remainder of this chapter and book contain pearls of wisdom from recovery, (actually throughout the whole book).

All choices and all decisions are important, or might be. Make fewer choices and more decisions.

"STOP GIVING AWAY YOUR POWER."

"A head full of AA and a belly full of alcohol don't mix."

"Don't change your goals to meet your habits, change your habits to meet your goals."

"Stop giving away your power."

"You can get (practically) anything you want if you help enough people get what they want."

"Takers eat better.

Givers sleep better."

"WATCH OUT FOR
THE ASSUMPTIONS."

"Assumptions make an ass out of you and me."

"Question authority....good.

Question everything (if possible).... very good.

Question nothing (being gullible — a serious character defect)....Very bad."

I recommend you start working on this one (being gullible) ASAP.

Try to question everything, if possible.

"STICK WITH THE WINNERS, NOT THE WHINERS."

"Stick with the winners, not the whiners."

"Upgrade your friends.

But help the newcomer; he or she may be your sponsor someday."

"In AA everyone is a student, and everyone is a teacher."

"There are no graduations in AA."

"There are no days off in AA."

"HALT"

"HALT:"

Don't get too hungry, angry, lonely or tired.

Hungry? Eat something, healthy (for you), if possible.

Angry? Do or say nothing if possible. "I'm an idiot when I'm angry."

Lonely? One solution, go to a meeting.

Tired? Get more and better sleep. Maybe take a nap.

"HALT."

"STAY IN THE MIDDLE OF THE PACK."

"Be a part of, rather than apart from."

"Stay in the middle of the pack to decrease your chances of getting picked off by the wolves and or the barflies."

"How do I accomplish that?"

Here are a few ideas:

Attend meetings; be the secretary, the literature person, the coffee maker, the greeter, etc. Go to conferences and picnics with speakers. Work with your sponsor and sponsees, and so on. (Sponsorship, like everything else in AA, is a suggestion only.)

WHEN REALISTIC, BELIEVE YOU CAN.

"Whether you believe you can or whether you believe you can't, you're right."

When realistic, believe you can.

"No is a complete sentence."

If you can't or don't say no when you need to, that's a character defect.

If you say no rudely, that's another character defect.

You can say: "No, thank you." You'll get over it.

"A PROGRAM FOR THE CROCKPOT."

One lady was being rushed by the meeting secretary to finish her share.

She said: "I don't accept that," and finished her share. I for one, admire that.

If possible:

Don't let other people rush you.

Don't rush yourself.

Don't rush other people.

"AA is not a program for the microwave. It's a program for the crockpot."

"ENJOY THE JOURNEY."

"It's not only about the destination. It's also about the journey. Enjoy the journey."

"Yesterday is gone and tomorrow will never come."

In recovery we switch habits, from alcohol and bars — for us, bad habits, addictions — to sobriety and meetings — for us, good habits, not addictions.

("An addiction is a bad habit.")

CREATE GOOD KARMA.

"Service with no strings attached ….good.

Service with no strings and you tell no one….very good."

If you do service with no strings and you tell no one, who pays you?

God, in God's time. (You've created good karma.)

"A BETTER SOLUTION FOR FEAR IS FAITH."

One of the big problems for people is fear, of course.

Alcohol is a common solution. (It's sometimes called liquid courage.)

One lady: "On alcohol, I'm wittier, prettier, and tittier."

"A better solution for fear is faith."

"First it's fun.

Then fun and problems.

Then just problems."

"FEAR THE ABSENCE OF FEAR."

No fear is also a problem, often leading to….disaster.

"The only thing to fear is the absence of fear."

"The solution:

Right-sized fear and faith."

Here's some not-so-swell news:

Our worst bottoms are probably yet to come, even while sober and in recovery. We get older. We make mistakes. Poop happens.

"A yet: You're eligible too."

ALCOHOL MAY STOP WORKING FOR YOU.

Here's more not-so-swell information which you may already know: Alcohol may eventually stop working for you.

If so, you would no longer be getting the buzz, but you would still crave it and still be killing yourself with it. You really would have a problem.

Your best move would probably be to get into recovery ASAP.

Actually, your best move is probably to get into recovery now, if you have a problem with alcohol.

THEY OFTEN SPEAK IN 3'S

People in recovery often speak in 3's.

Here are 17 examples:

"The speaker will share his or her experience, strength, and hope."

"The speaker's format:

What it was like, what happened, and what it is like now."

"We improve our physical, mental, and spiritual selves."

"Alcohol and recovery are cunning, baffling, and powerful."

"I CAME INTO NA PENNILESS, HOMELESS, AND JOBLESS."

"I came into NA penniless, homeless, and jobless. Now my job sends me all around the world."

"What is needed in recovery is honesty, open-mindedness, and willingness."

"Before recovery, we were restless, irritable, and discontent. In recovery, we may be restless, irritable, and discontent, but less."

"We used to be preoccupied with money, property, and prestige."

"KIND THOUGHTS, KIND WORDS, KIND DEEDS."

"Kind thoughts, kind words, kind deeds."

"We are recovering from a state of pitiful, incomprehensible, demoralization."

"God, grant me the serenity to accept the things I cannot change (usually people, places, and things), the courage...."

"We have experienced guilt, shame, and remorse."

"THINK, THINK, THINK."

"We need always maintain personal anonymity at the level of press, radio, and films (tradition 11, page 200)."

"We used to think we were hip, slick, and cool. Now we realize we weren't, and we don't want to be."

"Recovery will help us be happy, joyous, and free, or more so."

One lady: "On alcohol, I'm wittier, prettier, and tittier."

And of course: "Think, think, think."

FORGIVENESS IS MOSTLY ABOUT FORGIVING YOURSELF

Forgiveness is mostly about forgiving yourself. This is where a big part of your increased peace will come from. "How can I forgive myself?"

Start by making sure that you won't make the same mistake(s) again. (Do the best you can here.)

Study the amends you owe to others and to yourself.

What are the patterns, the character defects? Write them. Then, correct your character defects as best you can.

MINIMIZE
YOUR CHARACTER DEFECTS.

"So how do I correct my character defects?"

"Here's one idea:

For each character defect, write the opposite action(s). Practice and keep practicing the opposite action(s), if possible."

Suppose one character defect is haste. Some opposite actions:

"Slow down. Do less. Say less. Stop and think things through before and after. Don't react. Pray and meditate. Sleep on troubling issues, and so on."

TRUST YOUR INSTINCTS (USUALLY).

"What about forgiving others?"

Trust your instincts. Caution is good here.

"Fool me once, shame on you. Fool me twice shame on me."

Forgiveness is about forgiving yourself, or at least, it's a big part of it.

Needless to say, it's very important to identify your character defects. Keep looking for them. Write them. We'll come back to your character defects shortly.

"YOU FAIL TO PLAN,
YOU PLAN TO FAIL."

"Restraint and pausing….good.
Reacting and haste….bad."
"Speed kills."

"You fail to plan, you plan to fail."

The would haves, the could haves, and the should haves are often lumped together and considered to be wasted energy.

The would haves and could haves are not so helpful, but the should haves are good.

STUDY THE SHOULD HAVES.

Stop and think the should haves through to the end.

1) You may be able to at least partially clean up the mess, even now.

2) If or when the situation occurs again, you will be better prepared.

3) If a time machine comes for you, you will be better prepared.

"You fail to plan, you plan to fail."

INTERVENTIONS

WHAT ABOUT AN INTERVENTION?

Interventions have been successful and are a very good idea. So what in the heck is an intervention?

A group of concerned people close to the apparent addict surround him or her and say things like we care about you and it really looks like you are overdoing the drugs and or alcohol. They are apparently bringing you down and just might kill you.

We think you "better" do something about this (like AA, NA, or residential treatment) ASAP.

HE MAY THINK HE'S IN THE NILE.

One problem is....the person is probably in denial. (He may think he's in the Nile.) Also, he may be so stoned that he can't begin to find, get to, and sit through, an AA or NA meeting all by his lonesome.

Here's my original idea; I think it's original anyway:

Invite him to a place (perhaps a coffee shop) very close to an AA or NA speaker/discussion meeting already checked out, which will begin 15 to 20 minutes after he shows up, should he show up.

'HARD LOVE" MAY BE THE ANSWER.

After a few words, tell him he gets to go to the meeting. You will drive him there and you'll wait for him outside. Tell him to try to stay awake, and try to pay attention when he's inside. Dinner, $20, and a ride home await, should he survive the meeting. Tell him in advance, to try not to be too stoned and try to be a little presentable. You may need to repeat this process a few times.

And only give him money three times or so. You can imagine for yourself what he will be spending the money on.

It's called "hard love."

PATIENCE AND FAITH.

Take into account that some people will not succeed from AA and or NA out-patient alone. After perhaps a few days to three years, the next step, if the person agrees, is often a 28- or 30-day residential treatment program. And the person may need to go several times. (Sorry for the bad news.)

"Patience is a virtue," and faith can be very helpful.

After the residential program, 90 mee-tings in 90 days is practically a must.

Recovery, as you probably know, may be the difference between life and death.

THE OPIATES:
YOU'RE PLAYING WITH FIRE

I REPEAT:
YOU'RE PLAYING WITH FIRE.

If you are "hooked" on the opiates, you might be in real trouble!! Relying on obtaining your next fix from "the street" is very dangerous, as you probably know.

How do you know you won't be raped, and or robbed, and or killed at gunpoint or knifepoint? How do you know it's heroin, dilaudid, fentanyl, or vicodin, etc.? How do you know the dose? Sharing needles and or selling yourself sexually is practically asking for HIV, hepatitis C, herpes, gonorrhea, syphilis, sepsis or.... worse.

IF YOU'RE VERY LATE GETTING YOUR NEXT FIX, WELCOME TO HELL.

Your body normally produces its own opiates, but not when you are taking them at very high, nearly fatal daily doses. In that case, the body ceases all or nearly all production to try to prevent an "accidental" suicide.

If you don't get your next fix in time, welcome to hell: pain, paranoia, chills, and incontinence. Did I mention pain, or paranoia, or chills, or incontinence?

If relying on street opiates, a trip to the ER might be your best move.

PHYSICIAN-SUPERVISED PROGRAMS

Physician-supervised methadone and suboxone programs exist and are often good short-term, interim, or long-term solutions to ward off the brutal opiate withdrawal symptoms. Methadone, for example, is usually taken orally once or twice a day.

The physician can usually adjust the methadone dose based on the patient's sleep. If the patient's sleep is excessive, the dose probably should be lowered. If the patient wakes up early, pacing, unable to comfortably wait for the next dose, probably the dose should be raised.

CONSTIPATION IS NOT FUN.

While addicted to one of the opiates, the person will probably have another problem — constipation. Good luck with that one.

Methadone clinic humor or attempt anyway:

Prior to dropping off his 14-year-old daughter at school, the father stopped off at the methadone clinic for his daily dose of methadone. The physician told him he has good news and bad news. "The good news: Your last urine was clean for illegal drugs. The bad news: You're pregnant." (He had submitted his daughter's urine for his own.)

KICKING THE OPIATES.

If you are very late getting your next fix, or want to stop on your own, you will be kicking whichever opiate you're on, perhaps heroin. It takes a few weeks to kick the opiate cold turkey.

It's called kicking because countless people, while trying to withdraw from heroin, on the floor for long stretches of time, kicked at imaginary objects, like elephants or Martians. OK — probably imaginary.

OPIATE OVERDOSES.

The picture can get much worse. An all too common opiate story:

A rock star kicks heroin prior to his four-month world tour. The tour goes well and he returns with money to burn. He asks his pusher person to deliver a large quantity of the finest heroin, sparing no expense.

Frequently, the first time he shoots up, he fatally OD's. The problem: he cannot take the same high dose as before when he made practically no opiates for himself. The same applies to any opiate addict, off the opiates for a few days or longer.

MARIJUANA OVERDOSES.

Patient: "How is it that marijuana (pot) cannot kill me but the opiates can?"

Physician: "The part of the human brain which controls the breathing and heartbeat, the brainstem, has no canna-binoid (marijuana) receptors but has opiate receptors. The opiates depress the breathing and the heartbeat."

ABOUT AS SERIOUS
AS A HEART ATTACK.

Three last thoughts about opiate addiction:

1) Methadone and suboxone are very good prescription drugs for a lot of people.

2) Getting into recovery (NA, AA, or a residential program, etc.) ASAP is practically a must.

3) Opiate addiction may be about as serious as a heart attack.

THE FILMS, YOUTUBE, AND THE LITERATURE
(Writing and speaking in 3's is contagious.)

FILMS ABOUT RECOVERY.

By only watching the films, listening to the speakers on YouTube, and reading the literature, I think you would be seriously shortchanging yourself. Remember: "Meeting makers make it." But a lot of the above is helpful, excellent and enjoyable.

Here are my top eight film picks on recovery in chronological order:

"The Lost Weekend" — 1945

"The Man with the Golden Arm" (starring Frank Sinatra) — 1955

"Days of Wine and Roses" — 1962

"My Name is Bill W" — 1989

"Traffic" (starring Michael Douglas and Catherine Zeta-Jones) — 2000

"Flight" — 2010

"Bill W" — 2012

"Beautiful Boy" — 2018

SPEAKERS ABOUT RECOVERY.

Here's a good way to find an abundance of speakers on recovery: On YouTube, type in AA or NA speakers, etc. Listen.

Now, for the literature:

I suggest you start with the pamphlets. They are short, intended for the newcomer, and free or very inexpensive.

LITERATURE ABOUT RECOVERY.

The Grapevine, from AA, called "a meeting in print," comes out once a month. It is something you may like. Look it over during a meeting or two before or if you subscribe.

There are 1 and 1/2 must read and study AA books:

1) The Big Book *(Alcoholics Anony-mous).*

2) The steps portion of the 12 and 12 *(12 Steps and 12 Traditions).*

Read them, reread them, and go to book studies and step studies for them.

MORE ABOUT
RECOVERY LITERATURE.

I think you can put the rest of the books from AA on the back burner, at first, except for *Dr Bob and the Good Old Timers,* which is very underrated. Read this early on.

Narcotics Anonymous from NA and *Life with Hope* from MA are enlightening, if read, even if narcotics or marijuana are not your problems.

Go for the films, the speakers, and the literature at your leisure. "Easy does it." The price will be right or nearly always right.

And continue going to speaker/discussion meetings and doing the steps.

THE STEPS
OVERVIEW

(They are on page 199;
read and refer to them.)

HARDBALL.

What I have presented thus far is relatively light and easy. The steps aren't. They are hardball.

Read the following pages on the steps slowly and concentrate. After a while, start doing the steps. Start with pen to paper.

The steps will improve your life, give you peace, show you the direction home, and give you a new home.

"GO WITHIN OR GO WITHOUT."

From the steps, there is so much peace, so much self-improvement, so much improvement in our lives, that most people in recovery continue to do them indefinitely.

"More will be revealed."

"Good things happen to people who do the steps."

"Doing the steps — going within.
Not doing the steps — going without."

"MORE WILL BE REVEALED."

There are step study meetings where every week is the next step. After step 12 is step 1.

There are step study workshops, usually on one or both weekend days. There are 12 step workbooks. There is the steps portion of the 12 and 12, the book, *12 Steps and 12 Traditions*.

Check out the above suggestions for yourself.

"As you keep working on the steps, more will be revealed."

THE TWO UNOFFICIAL STEPS.

Officially there are 12 steps. Unofficially there are two more:

"Step zero: This shit has got to stop." ("I'm sick and tired of being sick and tired.")

Step 13: "Flirting with, or romance with someone in the rooms."

"Step zero ("This poop has got to stop.") will get you from the gutter onto the sidewalk.

Steps 1 to 12 will get you further and further away from the gutter.

Step 13 (flirting etc.) can go either way." You're on your own with this one.

CONSIDER
WORKING WITH A SPONSOR.

You can pick a sponsor and follow his or her guidance. I think when or if you pick a sponsor, you should aim for a fellow with years of sobriety and meetings, who you see regularly at meetings, who makes a lot of sense to you, and who you think you can get along with.

Men should usually sponsor men; women should usually sponsor women.

Try just about everything that seems productive, and go from there.

"EASY DOES IT."

Many people in recovery will tell the newcomer to get a sponsor and start on the steps ASAP.

I disagree. I think worrying about attending 90 meetings (mostly speaker/discussion) in 90 days, at 7 to 10 different places, worrying about not drinking, and worrying about your life, which might (might?) require some extra attention, will be enough for the first 1 and 1/2 to 3 months. "Easy does it."

"PEN TO PAPER"

I suggest you start the steps on your own, at your own pace. "Pen to paper."

If you're getting nowhere without a sponsor, get a sponsor. If you're getting nowhere with your first two to five sponsors, go back to working without a sponsor. Don't forget about the step studies, the step workshops, the steps portion of the 12 and 12, and so on.

And continue going to speaker/discussion meetings daily, if you can.

DON'T PROCRASTINATE TOO LONG.

Remember, the steps and sponsorship, like everything else in recovery, are suggestions only. Take what you like and leave the rest.

But take into account that most speakers at meetings, with years of sobriety, say that their sponsor plays a crucial role in their recovery. Often they say that their permanent sobriety did not begin until they connected with the right sponsor (for them).

And don't procrastinate too long before starting on the steps, if possible. They will set you free, improve your life, and give you peace.

THE SPONSOR'S JOB AT FIRST.

The sponsor's job at first is to get the sponsee through the steps and the Big Book. Pick your sponsor carefully. Perhaps take one to two weeks to decide. (Pausing and restraint are good.)

If it's not a good fit, change sponsors. They are supposed to support you, not give you poop, if you need or want a change. And thank the fellow for trying, if you think the fellow did.

"THE ONLY WAY TO DO THE STEPS WRONG IS NOT TO DO THEM."

Another dilemma:

Do the steps as is, or make some modifications, like rephrasing some of the steps, or changing the order.

My opinion or suggestion:

Do your own thing with the steps, including doing them precisely as written, if you are so inclined.

"The only way to do the steps wrong is not to do them."

Again: "The only way to do the steps wrong is not to do them."

ONE SPONSOR AND HER SPONSEES.

One sponsor has her sponsees do the steps any way they want. It's all OK with her.

But they must do the steps, report to her, read the literature, and of course, they must go to meetings.

If you decide to do step 5 as written, you don't have to pick your sponsor to tell the exact nature of your wrongs to.

You can pick a Buddhist monk in Tibet, a Chinese herbalist in Canada, a tuba player in New Zealand, and so on. But "don't pick the doorknob, it will turn on you."

THE STEPS
DOWN AND DIRTY

(They are on page 199;
read and refer to them.)

THE THREE SECTIONS OF THE STEPS.

WARNING: This chapter may begin to wear you down. If so, at any point, fast forward to the next chapter (Final Thoughts). You can come back to this chapter later, at least by when you start on the steps. For now, keep reading. There's important and helpful information in this chapter.

The 12 steps have often been broken down into 3 sections:

"Steps 1, 2, 3….We gave up (ICU).

Steps 4-9….We cleaned up (medical ward).

Steps 10, 11, 12….We grew up (out-patient)."

THE THREE SECTIONS OF THE STEPS (CONTINUED).

Steps 1, 2, 3 and steps 10, 11, 12:
Relatively easy.

Steps 4-9:

The six middle steps; relatively diffi-cult, but very, very important.

"Steps 1, 2, 3:

We gave up.

Step 1....We came.

Step 2....We came to.

Step 3....We came to believe."

ONE FELLOW'S STEP 1.

Step 1: We admitted we were powerless over our addiction — that our lives had become unmanageable. (Our addiction was and is very bad for us.)

One fellow says for step 1 that his addictions and character defects are and were very bad for him and that his life had become unmanageable.

Step 2: We came to believe that a power (not powder, power) greater than ourselves could restore us to sanity. (A higher power could be very beneficial and lifesaving.)

SURRENDERING
TO YOUR HIGHER POWER.

Step 3: We made a decision to turn our will (wills) and our lives over to the care of God as we understood Him.

(Many people think it should be as we understood God. Take into account that the 12 steps were written in 1938.)

Step 3 may be looked at as the surrendering to your higher power step.

Again, step 3 may be looked at as the surrendering to your higher power step.

"TAKE WHAT YOU LIKE AND LEAVE THE REST."

Whether your higher power is the program of AA or NA, etc. or not, take into account that not every suggestion, not every sentence in the literature, not everything you hear at meetings, perhaps not every step etc., is right on for you.

Probably most is, though. "Take what you like and leave the rest."

THE HOME STRETCH.

Steps 4-9: (the clean up steps, crucial) have been divided into:

Steps 4, 5, 6, 7: (about our character defects).

Steps 8, 9: (about our amends).

You're at the home stretch of the steps. Maybe get a glass of water. (Not vodka, water.)

"SEEK AND YE SHALL FIND."

Step 4 paraphrased:

We identified our character defects and character assets any way we could.

A big payoff comes from eliminating or minimizing our character defects. Ask yourself:

What are your character defects? Keep looking. "Seek and ye shall find. Pen to paper."

WHAT'S YOUR PART
IN THE MATTER?

"I have met the enemy and they is me."

In case you haven't noticed, there is one constant in the times you messed up (providing you think you did). You. You were involved. "It (supposedly) takes two to tango."

Worry about yourself first.

"If you are pointing your index finger at someone else, you have three fingers pointing back at you."

"I have met the enemy and they is me."

THE SPIRIT OF STEPS 5, 6, 7

Steps 5, 6, 7 I've combined. What is the spirit of steps 5, 6, 7? To eliminate or minimize our character defects.

Our character defects were usually good adaptations which turned on us, like the doorknob. (What is it with me and the doorknob?)

Here's one way to eliminate or minimize our character defects:

Prioritize them and for each one write the opposite and practice the opposite.

PRACTICE THE OPPOSITE.

Character defect   Opposite

Can't stop drinking — don't have the first drink.

Haste — slow down, think it through, pray, meditate, sleep on troubling issues, and so on.

Excessive ego or pride — humility.

Gullible — question everything if possible.

Big mouth — be quiet or say less.

"GOD HELPS THOSE WHO HELP THEMSELVES."

Again, so why did I put steps 5, 6, 7 together? Because, the spirit of steps 5, 6, 7 is right on: to eliminate or minimize our character defects.

"God won't do for me what I can do for myself."

"God helps those who help themselves."

FROM SIX TO 12 STEPS.

For the first 3 and 1/2 years of AA's existence, there were only six steps, from the Oxford Group. Bill W converted them to 12 steps in late 1938, in one night, as the story goes.

Many members were not happy with all of the changes and pleaded for various modifications. Bill made very few.

THE FASTER THE FELLOWSHIP COULD GROW.

Bill, God bless him, was busy writing the first edition of the Big Book, which would include the steps. The sooner the Big Book could come out, the sooner more alcoholics could get the message, and the faster the fellowship could grow.

The next two steps, steps 8 and 9, are about the amends.

WRITE YOUR LIST
AND MAKE YOUR AMENDS.

Step 8: We made a list of all persons we had harmed (including ourselves) and became willing to make amends to them all.

Write and study your list. You can learn a lot from it, like better understanding your character defects. "Pen to paper."

Step 9: We made direct amends to such people wherever possible, except when to do so would injure them or others.

Here's some good news:
We are included with the others.

"I'VE NEVER MADE AN AMEND THAT I'VE REGRETTED."

Once, and only once, I heard a fellow share that no one accepted his amends, including his parents and siblings. Everyone kicked him out and said don't come back.

Someone (me) had to ask him and did ask him: "Are you glad you made your amends?"

His answer: "Yes."

Several members: "I've never made an amend that I've regretted."

"PUT YOURSELF ON YOUR AMENDS LIST."

Newcomer: "Should I put myself on my amends list?"

Sober old timer: "Probably; and probably at the top, or near it."

Newcomer: "How do I make amends to myself?"

Sober old timer: "Here are a few ideas: Make sure you won't make the same mistake(s) again. (Do what you can). Eat well, take care of yourself, and make living amends (step 12)."

CONTINUE IMPROVING
YOUR CHARACTER DEFECTS.

Some people say that we should not make the amend unless we know we won't make the same mistake(s) again. Think about this one. You might find it helpful.

Study the amends you owe, including to yourself, and find and write the patterns, which include some of your character defects. It's probably the same character defects over and over.

After that, do what you can to eliminate or minimize them.

HE IMPROVED HIMSELF
AND HIS LIFE.

One member discovered that practically all the amends he owes, including to himself, are due to haste.

By slowing down, thinking things through, praying, meditating, and sleeping on troubling issues, etc., he improved himself and his life.

"LIVING AMENDS."

There are amends you cannot or should not make. The person may be deceased, cannot be located, or making the amend will harm them or others. (You are a part of the others.)

You can always write letters from your heart and burn them. You can make "living amends" (step 12) by being of service and practicing the principles in all of your affairs.

"DON'T UNDERESTIMATE STEP 10."

"Steps 10, 11, 12:

The growth steps."

Step 10: We continued to take personal inventory and when we were wrong, promptly admitted it. (And if possible, corrected it, after thinking it through.)

"If I think I might owe someone an apology or an amend, I just make it, if I can. It's one less thing to worry about later."

"Don't underestimate step 10."

PRAYER AND MEDITATION.

Step 11: We sought through prayer and meditation....

Many fellows say:

"Praying is talking to God.

Meditating is listening to God."

If your higher power is the program of AA or NA, etc., at a meeting, you can go with:

When speaking, you are praying.

When listening, you are meditating.

SPIRITUAL AWAKENINGS.

Step 12: Having had a spiritual awakening (our spirits awaken) as a result of these steps, we tried to carry this message to addicts (we were of service), and to practice these principles in all our affairs (we were good people).

Step 12 may be thought of as the living amends step.

Again, step 12 may be thought of as the living amends step.

Here's another way to define a spiritual awakening:

We wake up "clean and serene." What a concept.

FINAL THOUGHTS

RECOMMENDED ROCK SONGS AND FILMS.

I've already recommended three rock songs for you to listen to. I couldn't help but add Elvis Presley's "Are You Lonesome Tonight?"

 Type and watch on YouTube:

Elvis Are You Lonesome Tonight?

Harrison All Things Must Pass.

McCartney Let It Be.

Mellencamp Like a Rolling Stone.

For my top eight film picks, see page 151. Watch. Start with "The Man with the Golden Arm" or "Traffic."

THE KING OF ROCK AND ROLL

As you probably know, people still miss Elvis and still make pilgrimages to Graceland, his home in Memphis, Tennessee, open to the public. Graceland is the second most visited home in the United States, second only to the White House.

Watch him when he really had his mojo going, from 1955 to 1957, off drugs, before he was drafted, well before he died of a multiple prescription drug overdose (including Quaaludes) at age 42 in 1977.

Elvis is still "the king of rock and roll," and I'm not alone with that opinion.

A BELOVED PRAYER.

The Serenity Prayer:

God grant me the serenity to accept the things I cannot change (usually people, places, and things), the courage (power) to change the things I can (usually me), and the wisdom to know the difference.

(Attributed to Reinhold Niebuhr)

A VERY INFLUENTIAL SPEECH.

The title of this book, *Give Me Recovery or Give Me Death,* is a slight deviation from Patrick Henry's words "Give me liberty or give me death," first delivered at the Second Virginia Convention on March 20, 1775 at St. John's Episcopal Church. In the following year, 1776, the Declaration of Independence was signed and the American Revolution began.

THE CONCLUSION
OF PATRICK HENRY'S SPEECH.

Patrick Henry — May 29, 1736 to June 6, 1799 — attorney, planter, and orator.

The conclusion of his famous speech:

"Is life so dear, or peace so sweet, as to be purchased at the price of chains or slavery?

Forbid it, almighty God. I know not what course others may take, but as for me, give me liberty or give me death."

"EASY DOES IT."

If you are new, welcome to recovery. Perhaps next, attend a few AA and NA speaker/discussion meetings. "Keep coming back."

If you're not new, "Keep coming back."

Either way, "You have a second chance at a first-class life."

"Stop giving away your power."

"Easy does it."

"Progress, not perfection."

"Meeting makers make it."

I repeat, "Meeting makers make it."

"Stick with the winners."

"Enjoy the journey."

THE 12 STEPS AND 12 TRADITIONS OF NA

PERMISSION TO REPRINT.

Taken from the book *Narcotics Anonymous,* 6th edition.

THE 12 STEPS OF NA.

1. We admitted we were powerless over our addiction, that our lives had become unmanageable. 2. We came to believe that a Power greater than ourselves could restore us to sanity. 3. We made a decision to turn our will and our lives over to the care of God *as we understood Him.* 4. We made a searching and fearless moral inventory of ourselves. 5. We admitted to God, to ourselves, and to another human being the exact nature of our wrongs. 6. We were entirely ready to have God remove all these defects of character. 7. We humbly asked Him to remove our shortcomings. 8. We made a list of all persons we had harmed, and became willing to make amends to them all. 9. We made direct amends to such people wherever possible, except when to do so would injure them or others. 10. We continued to take personal inventory and when we were wrong promptly admitted it. 11. We sought through prayer and meditation to improve our conscious contact with God *as we understood Him,* praying only for knowledge of His will for us and the power to carry that out. 12. Having had a spiritual awakening as a result of these steps, we tried to carry this message to addicts, and to practice these principles in all our affairs.

THE 12 TRADITIONS OF NA.

1. Our common welfare should come first; personal recovery depends upon NA unity. 2. For our group purpose there is but one ultimate authority- a loving God as He may express Himself in our group conscience. Our leaders are but trusted servants; they do not govern. 3. The only requirement for NA membership is a desire to stop using. 4. Each group should be autonomous except in matters affecting other groups or NA as a whole. 5. Each group has but one primary purpose-to carry its message to the addict who still suffers. 6. An NA group ought never endorse, finance or lend the NA name to any related facility or outside enterprise, lest problems of money, property and prestige divert us from our primary purpose. 7. Every NA group ought to be fully self-supporting, declining outside contributions. 8. Narcotics Anonymous should remain forever nonprofessional, but our service centers may employ special workers. 9. NA, as such, ought never to be organized, but we may create special boards or committees directly responsible to those they serve. 10. Narcotics Anonymous has no opinion on outside issues; hence the NA name ought never to be drawn into public controversy. 11. Our public relations policy is based on attraction rather than promotion; we need always maintain personal anonymity at the level of press, radio and films. 12. Anonymity is the spiritual foundation of all our Traditions, ever reminding us to place principles before personalities.

THE DIRECTION HOME

THE DIRECTION HOME

THE DIRECTION HOME

Printed in the United States
By Bookmasters